50 THING
BOOK SERIES
REVIEWS FROM READERS

I recently downloaded a couple of books from this series to read over the weekend thinking I would read just one or two. However, I so loved the books that I read all the six books I had downloaded in one go and ended up downloading a few more today. Written by different authors, the books offer practical advice on how you can perform or achieve certain goals in life, which in this case is how to have a better life.

The information is simple to digest and learn from, and is incredibly useful. There are also resources listed at the end of the book that you can use to get more information.

50 Things To Know To Have A Better Life: Self-Improvement Made Easy!

Author Dannii Cohen

This book is very helpful and provides simple tips on how to improve your everyday life. I found it to be useful in improving my overall attitude.

50 Things to Know For Your Mindfulness & Meditation Journey
Author Nina Edmondso

Quick read with 50 short and easy tips for what to think about before starting to homeschool.

50 Things to Know About Getting Started with Homeschool by Author Amanda Walton

I really enjoyed the voice of the narrator, she speaks in a soothing tone. The book is a really great reminder of things we might have known we could do during stressful times, but forgot over the years.

Author Harmony Hawaii

There is so much waste in our society today. Everyone should be forced to read this book. I know I am passing it on to my family.

50 Things to Know to Downsize Your Life: How To Downsize, Organize, And Get Back to Basics

Author Lisa Rusczyk Ed. D.

Great book to get you motivated and understand why you may be losing motivation. Great for that person who wants to start getting healthy, or just for you when you need motivation while having an established workout routine.

50 Things To Know To Stick With A Workout: Motivational Tips To Start The New You Today

Author Sarah Hughes

50 THINGS TO KNOW ABOUT PLAYING GUITAR

The Primer On WHAT To Know,
Before You Start Learning It!

Vince Elhalawany

Cover designed by: Ivana Stamenkovic
Cover Image: https://pixabay.com/photos/guitar-classical-
guitar-756326/

CZYK Publishing Since 2011.

50 Things to Know

Lock Haven, PA
All rights reserved.
ISBN: 9798597885179

50 THINGS TO KNOW ABOUT PLAYING GUITAR

BOOK DESCRIPTION

Have you ever wanted to learn to play guitar, but found the subject too complex and unapproachable? Are You teaching yourself through youtube and online programs, but find that the lack of structure or organization leaves you learning concepts that are useful, yet disjointed and all over the place? Do You find academic music theory jargon to be overly complex, and just too much to handle?If you answered yes to any of these questions then this book is for you...

50 Things To Know About Playing Guitar by author Vince Elhalawany offers an approach to learning the guitar in an easy common sense style. Most books on learning guitar tell you to learn tons of scales with no context and very complex music theory. Although, there's nothing wrong with that, based on knowledge from the world's leading experts and musicians; there is a better way. The world of guitar, and music in general becomes much more palatable, when taken from a simple, yet organized approach.

In these pages you'll discover exactly what you need to learn; before you begin down the lifelong path of your guitar and musical journey. This book will help you in that it will give you a structured order of concepts to learn, and a more specific order in how they should be approached. This book WILL NOT teach you to play your instrument, no book can, only live and video lessons can teach you that. What this book will do is give you a primer and structure so that you CAN learn effectively.

By the time you finish this book; you will know what you need to learn and look for in an order that makes cohesive sense. So grab YOUR copy today. You'll be glad you did.

TABLE OF CONTENTS

DEDICATION

To Justin & Julianna Maness and John Falt, three righteous dudes who enrich my life, and the lives of others.

ABOUT THE AUTHOR

Vince Elhalawany is a writer, guitarist, and a poet. He has been studying guitar for over 10 years and is mostly self taught; which is exactly why he jumped at the chance to write this book. Many of us especially, in the age of Youtube and the internet are self taught. His goal with this book is to help you avoid the numerous pitfalls he faced while learning in the wild-west environment that is the internet.

Currently he is free-lance writing while exploring the great outdoors of The United States.

INTRODUCTION

*"Most people are prisoners,
thinking only about the future or
living in the past. They are not in
the present, and the present is
where everything begins."*

-Carlos Santana

Learning to play guitar was one of the toughest things I have ever had to do. It challenged me mentally, spiritually, and psychologically. Sticking to a practice routine is one of the main things which brought discipline and order into my life. There were many pitfalls I encountered as a beginner in the 21st century; mainly information overload, and disjointed concepts. I partly taught myself, but also sought out the help of others when I needed to. My goal with this book is to try to give you structure, and help you to avoid many of the mistakes I made. I have split the book up into five equal parts: basics, music theory, practice tips, electric guitar tips, and playing with others. Before you read this book you must understand one thing: there is no book on earth that will teach you to play guitar, or any other instrument for that matter. This book is meant as a guide, and a primer to light your way through uncharted territory; it is not meant to be a substitute for practice or musical lessons. This book also follows a particular order; try your best to follow it in the order it was written. I sincerely hope that reading this book will give you as much joy as it has given me to write it.

1. PLAYING GUITAR IS ABOUT BRINGING BEAUTY INTO THE WORLD

Playing guitar is not about being the most technically skilled; most songs that hit it big used simple 1,4,5 chord progressions, and simple melodies. Guitar is not about being the loudest person in the room either; it is not about showing up with a 150 watt Marshall head and matching cabs. Some of the greatest songs ever recorded were done using small 5-10 watt amps. Playing guitar is a spiritual journey; one that is about patience, learning, mastery, and beauty. Being a guitarist is very much like being a martial artist; it takes discipline, study, and the sharpening of the senses. Much like the martial artists, and warrior poets of old, the guitarist is conscious of bringing beauty into the world. Tip number one is to approach this as a spiritual pursuit; to approach guitar as a mechanism to bring truth, and beauty into the world.

2. PATIENCE YOUNG GRASSHOPPER

The first time I picked up a guitar and tried to play my first chord, which was an open A Major chord, I thought the entire thing was impossible. I remember the exact thoughts I had:

"How does anyone do this?"

"My fingers just cannot move in this way."

"What is that horrible noise interference coming from the amplifier?

"Maybe this just is not for me, I was not born with the musical gift."

I also made the dreaded statement nearly every beginner guitarist makes: "maybe my hands/fingers are just too small." After years of playing I can tell you that those statements and questions were complete nonsense. I can pretty much guarantee, if you have not had these exact thoughts already, you will when you start learning. I am here to tell you that having these thoughts is perfectly alright, natural, and everyone has them when they first start. The moral of this tip is patience. Just be patient and practice daily for a minimum of 30 minutes, and I promise you will start to see results. Your finger dexterity, rhythm, and picking will all get better with consistent, and dedicated practice.

3. PLAYING GUITAR WILL HURT AT FIRST

The first time I tried to play a chord on guitar it hurt! Not just a little either, it hurt a great deal, certainly enough to say something about it here. When you first start playing your fingers are going to hurt; you are not the first, and you certainly won't be the last! However; there is good news: your fingers will stop hurting the more you play. Why is this the case? The more you play guitar the thicker the calluses on your fingers will grow. These calluses are going to be your saving grace. No guitarist can play effectively without the thick calluses on the tips of their fingers.Make sure you spend time every single day practicing, so your calluses grow nice and thick.

4. KEEP THE NAILS ON YOUR FRETTING HAND COMPLETELY TRIMMED

Most of us will be fretting the strings with the left hand, and picking with our right hands. If you are left handed, the opposite will be true for you, you will fret with your right hand and pick with your left. The nails on your fretting hand must be completely trimmed back, so the free edge of the nail (the white part) is completely, or very nearly gone. This is EXTREMELY important; you cannot properly fret notes and chords without doing this. The strings will buzz, mute, and just sound terrible. I cannot stress this enough: keep the nails on your fretting hand trimmed.

5. FRET NOTES WITH THE BALL OF YOUR FINGERTIPS, NOT THE PAD

Hold out your arm out straight from your body, with your palm facing the ceiling. Next, I want you to bend your arm so that it makes a 90 degree angle. Now, bend your wrist toward your face, so that your hand rests at another 90 degree angle. You see the tips of your fingers staring you in the face? Good! These tips (the ball) are what you should be fretting notes with; do not use the padding of your finger. Many guitarists will use the padding and other parts of their fingers to barre and mute strings, but we will get to that later. For now, just remember that you should be fretting every note with the balls of your fingers, the tips of your fingers, never the pad.

6. TRY TO ALWAYS PRACTICE ON ACOUSTIC

Practicing on an acoustic guitar is a much harder workout for your fingers than playing an electric guitar. The strings on an acoustic guitar are much thicker, and hold far more tension than electric guitar strings. This will do wonders for building your calluses, improving your finger dexterity, and strengthening your picking hand.

7. LEARN TO PALM MUTE EARLY ON

I cannot stress the importance of palm muting enough. Palm muting is the act of using the flesh on your picking hand to mute the strings you are NOT playing. Palm muting is accomplished by resting your picking hand close to the bridge of your guitar, and moving it closer to the strings you want to mute. If you do not do this, other strings will ring out as you play, and it will make everything sound 'muddy' and noisy. Palm muting matters far more on electric guitar; due to the extreme sensitivity of the magnetic pickups present in the instrument. I strongly recommend you learn palm muting very early on; it is essential for good technique. Go watch a video on palm muting, or seek a live lesson from a guitar teacher. No book or simple diagram can really teach you how to do this.

8. THE STANDARD TUNING ON A GUITAR IS E-A-D-G-B-E

Standard tuning is what most guitars are tuned to. This means that the thickest string is tuned to the note

11

'E.' The thick 'E' string is also known as the 6th string. As we go up in pitch, towards the floor, and towards the thinnest string we go down in number. The A string is the 5th string, the D string is the 4th string, the G is the 3rd, the B is the 2nd, and the thinnest string, the high 'e' is the 1st string.

9. LEARN TO READ GUITAR TABS AND CHORD CHARTS

These are the absolute beginners tools that will get you through your first lessons in chords, scales, simple riffs, and songs. Guitar Tabs are written on a staff consisting of 6 lines; each line is meant to represent one string on your guitar. There is a catch though: tabs are staffed according to pitch, so what does this mean for you? Tabs are written so that the lowest string, the 6th 'E' string, is on the bottom of the tab staff. The highest line of the staff represents the high pitched 'e' string. In my experience this took some getting used to, and was extremely unnatural at first. You will see numbers on the tab staff; these numbers represent the fret you are supposed to place your finger on to play that particular note on that particular string. Chord charts look like boxed matrices. Each line that goes north to south represents an individual string. The lines oriented east to west create boxes which represent individual frets. The beauty of chord charts is that they are extremely intuitive: you will notice that they look just like your fretboard! Chord charts will have dots indicating where you should place your fingers to make that particular chord. The dots will almost always have numbers inside them; these numbers represent which finger you use on that particular note. Your index finger is number one, your middle finger is number two, your ring finger is number three, finally your pinky is number four. The north-south line that is all the way to the left indicates the thickest string; the lowest pitched 'E' string. The north-south line that is all the way to the right, represents the thinnest string, the high 'e' string.

10. LEARN YOUR OPEN CHORDS!

Let's be real. You came here because you want to PLAY guitar, you want to make music. The first thing I recommend you learn are your open chords. There are several reasons for this: first, they are the simplest and easiest chords to learn; everyone has to start somewhere. The second reason is that learning these chords will serve as your introductory lessons to help your finger dexterity and thicken up those calluses! Lastly, learning these chords will keep you engaged and motivated enough to continue learning. You want something fun to keep you entertained through the harder, more tedious, parts of learning guitar.

11. THERE ARE SEVEN LETTERS AND 12 NOTES IN WESTERN MUSIC

Those letters are: A, B, C, D, E, F, and G. The 12 notes of the western chromatic scale are as follows: A, A#, B, C, C#, D, D#, E, F, F#, G, and G#. Notice there are five notes in between some of these letters known as sharps or flats. Sharps are denoted using a pound sign symbol (#). Flats are denoted using a lowercase letter 'b'. I want you to start thinking about sharps and flats as relative terms that describe the same note. Let me give you an example: A sharp (A#) is the exact same note as B flat (Bb). Both A# and Bb are describing the note which is located in between A and B. The general rule is this: when going up in pitch (A to B) use sharp signs to label the in-between notes, but when going down in pitch (B to A) use flat symbols to label the in-between notes. Here is an illustration of this concept:

A# = Bb

C# = Db

D# = Eb

F# = Gb

G# = Ab

12. BASIC MUSICAL TERMS

Almost every single song you have ever heard contains these five basic elements: melody, chords, beat, rhythm and lyrics. Melody refers to notes played one at a time; the major scale is an example of a basic melody. Chords are two or more notes played at the same time; chords give an underlying structure to the music. Most chords are composed of 3 or more notes; with the exception of power chords and double stops. You may also hear chords referred to as harmony. The beat is the pulse or heartbeat of the music; this is a percussive element almost always fulfilled by the drums. Rhythm is what gives movement and flow to melodic and harmonic elements. Finally, lyrics are the words or poetry found within a song. Another essential term to know is 'octave'; an octave is the same note vibrating at exactly double or half the value of the original note. Let me give you an example: suppose an 'A' note vibrates at 440hz an octave up (higher pitch) would vibrate at 880hz. Using that same original 'A' note at 440hz an octave down (lower pitch) would be 220hz. You do not need to know the hertz values for any notes; I am simply using the numbers to illustrate the concept of an octave to you. There are more musical terms to learn of course, but know these six for sure when starting out.

13. LEARN YOUR INTERVALS

Intervals are the distances between any two notes on any musical instrument, and are the basic building blocks of music. Intervals come in three different qualities: major, minor, and perfect. Major intervals are denoted with a capital 'M', minor intervals are denoted by a lowercase 'm', or the flat symbol (b). Perfect intervals with the letter 'P.' Major intervals usually sound happy, and bouncy; minor intervals sound melancholy or a little sad. Perfect intervals sound extremely stable, and are usually good places to resolve (end) a musical phrase. There are only

three perfect intervals: the perfect fourth, the perfect
fifth, and the octave. The closest interval is the minor
2nd interval (m2); if you play a note on the fifth fret
of any string, and then play the note on the sixth fret
then you have played a minor 2nd interval. The
distance between frets right next to each other is
known as a half step. The interval right after a minor
2nd is the major 3rd; a major 3rd sounds bright and
happy, and skips a fret, so a note played on the fifth
fret of any string followed by a note played on the
seventh fret of that same string represents a major 3rd
interval. This distance is known as a whole step. The
further away you get from the root note the larger the
interval distance is said to be; larger interval distances
require the use of multiple strings. Once you reach the
perfect fourth interval, the distance between the notes
becomes uncomfortable, and impractical to play on
one single string; this is where interval shapes come
in. I will post a link to a youtube source that contains
a short class on intervals, and interval geometry
sheets.You need to not only be able to recognize the
interval shapes on the guitar fretboard, but also be
able to recognize them by ear. The best way to do this
is by using solfege syllables to sing the intervals as
you play them; the solfege syllables are: do, ra, re,
me, mi, fa, fi, sol, le, la, te, ti, do. Each of these

solfege syllables corresponds to a particular interval; do a quick internet search for a solfege syllables to intervals translation chart. I also highly recommend getting an ear training app for your phone; there are many and all cost roughly $3. Make sure you are doing daily interval practice for about 15 minutes; I cannot stress to you how important this is. I will include a reference list of all 12 musical intervals below:

1- minor 2nd (m2) - Dissonant and very tense sounding.

2- Major 2nd (M2)- Bland, 'happy birthday' starts with a Major 2nd interval.

3- Minor 3rd (m3)- soft and sad.

4- Major 3rd (M3)- Bright and happy.

5- Perfect 4th(P4)- Stable and consonant.

6- Tritone   (b5)- Extremely disturbing, very dissonant.

7- Perfect 5th (P5)- Extremely stable, many chords progressions resolve to the 5th.

8- minor 6th   (m6)- Sounds dissonant and unstable.

9- Major 6th   (M6)- Bright and has a chime like quality.

10- minor 7th (m7)- Has a blues like sound to it.

11- Major 7th- (M7)- Disjointed and dissonant.

12- Octave   (P8)- Stable, and extremely consonant.

14. LEARN THE MAJOR SCALE

The major scale is the most important scale in western music; why is it the most important scale in western music? The major scale is the scale from which all other modes, and scales are derived. Understanding the major scale formula is a must; the major scale formula is: 1,2,3,4,5,6,7. The first note is the root note, the major scale contains only major and perfect intervals, and it is also known as the Ionian mode. People will say that the major scale sounds bright and happy, but it has limited application outside of using it as a base formula for modes. Understanding the major scale is more about using it as a concept to understand more complex concepts. There are very few times where you will actually use a major scale in playing or performance.

15. MEMORIZE THE NOTES ON THE 5TH AND 6TH STRINGS

Most chords you encounter and most of the scales you will see have their root notes on the 5th, or 6th string. This means that the chord or scale is starting off on a note on one of those two strings. There is also one added benefit to doing this: the notes on the high 'e' string are the exact same as the notes on the low 'E' string, so memorizing the notes on the 5th and 6th strings actually gives you an understanding of half the guitar fretboard. This is not as hard as you think; beginning on the 12th fret of each string the note names repeat again. Let's assume your guitar is in standard tuning (EADGBE); the notes on the 12 fret are also EADGBE.

16. LEARN YOUR BARRE CHORD SHAPES

Barre chords were one of the absolute hardest things I had to learn as a guitarist; they take a great deal of hand strength to pull off properly. These chords get their name from the placement of your 1st finger (index) on the fretboard to press down on all 5 or 6 strings of the guitar. While your index finger is firmly pressed against the appropriate strings your remaining fingers will fret the notes appropriate to that barre chord shape. These chords have so much utility for rhythm guitar playing; no one wants to switch between open chords due to efficiency and voicing reasons. The second reason for learning barre chord shapes is arguably more important; barre chord shapes will demystify many things about the neck, and interval placement. Recognizing the patterns and shapes of these barre chords will help you immensely; trust me on this, and go fetch a barre chord shape sheet from the web.

17. LEARN THE MINOR PENTATONIC SCALE

The minor pentatonic scale is the go to scale for most guitarists. This scale is used all over blues, rock, country, and pop music. Pentatonic scales each contain only 5 notes: 1(root), m3, p4, p5, and an m7 interval. In my opinion they are the easiest, and most versatile scales to understand. As you advance in your guitar journey you will need other scales; do not just be the player that relies on pentatonics, but

understanding them will absolutely give you the
confidence and competence to go play with others.

18. CHORD TONES AND WHY YOU SHOULD KNOW THEM

Chord tones are the notes within the particular
chord that the rhythm guitarist is playing. Knowing
where these notes are is essential to good lead
playing. An excellent rule of thumb is this: start and
land back on the root note of the chord the other
guitarist is playing within the scale you are using.
Each scale position will have two octaves of the same
exact notes you can choose from, as long as you
begin on the root note of the chord you can play all
the notes of the scale, so long as you land on the root
note again by the end of the chord. Let the notes
breathe as you are playing, but knowing where these
chord tones are will make your playing sound
authoritative.

19. MODES

Modes are a more advanced musical concept; we have already learned one mode: the Ionian mode, or major scale. Every single mode is derived from the major scale using formulas specific to that mode. The modes are: Ionian, Dorian, Phyrgian, Lydian, Mixolydian, Aeolian, and Locrian. Each mode begins on a different degree of the major scale; the Dorian mode begins on the 2nd degree of the major scale, the Phyrigian on the 3rd degree, the Lydian on the 4th degree, and so on. Modes each have a distinctive flavor; the Phyrigian mode is dark and exotic sounding, the Aeolian mode (natural minor scale) sounds sad, the Mixoldian mode is a primary feature of AC/DC's music.

20. LEARNING ARPEGGIOS

Arpeggios can be played in one of two ways: playing the notes within a chord you are holding down one at a time, or finding those notes in different positions on the fretboard. Both are important, but I want you to focus on the latter. Here is a hint: everything you have been learning so far: the notes on the two lowest strings, intervals, barre chord shapes will all help you out here tremendously. Arpeggios are pretty much chord tones; when people talk about 'playing from the chord' this is usually what they mean.

21. STRUCTURED PRACTICE

By now I have given you a multitude of things to practice and study. Do you feel overwhelmed? I did too. The ideal practice session is roughly 3 hours per day, and you would practice 6 days out of the week. I would recommend that your practice sessions break down into something like this: 1 hour and 45 minutes of whatever song, riffs or chord concepts you are learning, 1 hour of scale practice, and 15 minutes of ear training. There will be days where you cannot do this; if that is the case then do at least 30 minutes split evenly between scale practice and ear training. Make sure you either learn the music theory you need for that particular lesson/song/concept either at the beginning of your practice session, or set aside 2 hours weekly to review these concepts.

22. SEEK PROFESSIONAL HELP IF YOU NEED TO

Youtube is a powerful platform and an excellent learning tool. I will say one thing though: learning to play guitar through youtube is extremely frustrating. Do not misunderstand me; there is plenty of great information on Youtube, and you should use it just don't rely on it. The problem with Youtube is that there is too much information, and so much of it is disjointed. Instead try joining an online program with guided structured practice, or find a guitar teacher in real life. Structure to your practice is probably more important than the practice itself; guitar and music in general are both extremely broad topics.

23. DO NOT PRACTICE CONCEPTS IN ISOLATION

This tip plays off of the previous tip; do not practice concepts in a disjointed way. Everything you will learn on guitar is connected. Concepts are meant to flow together seamlessly, and at first you will have no choice but to learn things bit by bit. Once you feel confident that you have some rudimentary understanding of the most basic things, start practicing those things all together. One of the best ways to do this is to transcribe songs by ear; this means listening to a song, and trying to work it out based on what you hear. Ear training goes a long way here, but learning songs while being mindful of the musical concepts within them also helps. Do not simply continue to learn using tabs once you get out of the beginning phases.

24. MOST SONG BOOKS AND TABS CONTAIN CONFUSING ERRORS

It's one of the best kept secrets in the world of musical instruction: most song books and tabs contain glaring errors. This occurs for two main reasons: copyright, and the differences in the human ear. We all hear things differently, and if you are transcribing music you will write it down the way you hear it, not necessarily the way the original composer wrote it. For a beginner this will definitely be confusing, it was for me! No one told me either; I just had to find out for myself. Beginner guitarists need tabs for their intro lessons, but once beyond the intro phase consider ditching tabs altogether.

25. PRACTICE WITH A METRONOME

Timing matters so much in music; if you remember rhythm and beat are among the most essential musical concepts. One of the best ways to work on your timing is to practice with a metronome; a metronome is a device which keeps time through a series of audible clicks. My advice is to download one to your smartphone; I personally use the pro metronome app, but you should use whichever one you feel the most comfortable with. These metronomes are about $2-3 each.

26. PRACTICE SCALES OVER A BACKING TRACK

One of the biggest problems most beginners face is the lack of musicality in their scales and melodic playing. This was one of the things which plagued me in the beginning, but I got over it by practicing scales and melodic concepts over backing tracks. Scales often sound bland and unmusical by themselves, so try playing the same scales over a backing track to get some harmonic and rhythmic movement in there.

27. BUY A LOOPER PEDAL

A looper pedal is a small device which either sits on your pedalboard at the end, or as a completely separate unit placed after the pedalboard and before the amp. These little pedals record whatever you are playing on guitar, and loop it over and over again through your amplifier. I strongly suggest that you eventually buy one of these for practice purposes. Eventually, you will either tire of backing tracks, or have trouble finding the one you want. You are also going to want to practice the riffs, chord progressions, and songs that you or a bandmate have created…..not someone else's.

28. RECORD YOURSELF AND LISTEN TO IT

I would strongly recommend that you record your playing from time to time; doing so will help you to correct errors and inspire you to play more. The gold standard for recording software is Apple Protools, but if you do not have it, or cannot afford it use your smartphone to record. A word of caution though: smartphones and small personal recorders do not capture anything in high fidelity, but if you have no other choice use the phone or a personal recorder.

29. GET GUITAR PRO 7 OR MUSESCORE 3

These pieces of software are among the most underrated, yet powerful tools available to guitarists today. Both programs allow you to easily transcribe musical ideas to paper, but that is not where they shine. Each program allows you to play back what you have written down; this can help you to create backing tracks, understand rhythm and timing better, understand how to read standard musical notation, and a whole host of other things. I use Musescore, but would recommend Guitarpro 7; Musescore is free, but Guitarpro 7 is far more robust.

30. PRACTICE STANDING UP, OR ON AN ARMLESS BAR STOOL

This may sound silly, but practice either standing up, or in an armless bar stool. Every gig you will ever do will either be standing up, or sitting in an armless bar stool. Do not sit on the ground cross legged and practice, do not sit on your bed and practice, do not sit in a regular chair and practice. Doing any of these things usually messes with proper arm position on guitar, and will stifle your playing. Even using the bar stool all the time is not good, as you will notice that standing up and playing is a little different than sitting down and playing.

31. PLAY YOUR ELECTRIC GUITAR OUT OF A TUBE AMP

Don't take my word for it; go and find a professional guitarist, and ask them if you should use a solid-state amplifier or a tube amplifier. Tube amplifiers produce sounds which are naturally pleasing to the ear. This difference in sound quality is due to the harmonic qualities of vactrol radio tubes, as well as the natural clipping and organic overdrive of the tubes. Tube amplifiers are typically more expensive than their solid-state counterparts, but are worth every penny. You can use solid-state pedals, most pedals are solid-state, but avoid using solid-state amplifiers.

32. SINGLE-COIL OR HUMBUCKING PICKUPS?

Pickups are magnetic devices found near the bridge and neck of an electric guitar; they 'pick up' the vibrations from your guitar strings and transfer them via cable to your amp. In the world of electric guitar there are two main choices of pickups: single-coil and humbucker. Single-coil pickups were invented before humbucking pickups, and sound thinner; many guitarists describe them as having a 'chimey' sound. They sound beautiful, but have one major flaw: single-coil pickups are sensitive to all manner of electromagnetic interference. Everything from flat-panel televisions to neon lights can be picked up by single-coils and will cause a loud hum in your guitar signal. There are many ways around this: RFI shielding, standing at certain angles, turning off the interfering devices, but this interference is an issue you should be aware of. The most common types of single-coil guitars are the Fender Stratocaster, and the Fender Telecaster. Humbucking pickups were invented after the single-coil, and sought to remedy the problem of this electromagnetic interference by having two opposite-wound coils in the pickup. Humbucker pickups sound 'fatter' and more full-bodied; most Gibson guitars feature humbucker pickups. There is no right or wrong choice here; the pickups you choose will largely be determined by your own unique taste.

33. DIALING IN YOUR SOUND

Let me tell you a secret: most amplifiers only sound good at one volume setting; this volume setting is known as 'the sweet spot.' The sweet spot is the spot where your amplifier is on the edge of breakup and distortion. Want to know another secret? Most of the amps you will ever use have a sweet spot around 5 or 6. The secret to a big soaring guitar tone is to turn the volume on your amplifier to 5 or 6, but turn your guitar volume down to 2 or 3. Do not turn your amplifier all the way up to 11, and do not turn your guitar all the way up to 10 either. Once you have dialed in your sound use overdrive and distortion pedals to achieve high gain breakup,crunch, or distortion.

34. HEADROOM AND DISTORTION

The lower the headroom on your amplifier the easier it will be to distort or push into overdrive. The higher the headroom the more difficult it will be to push the amp into distortion territory. Once again, there is really no right or wrong way here; there is only personal preference. Most guitarists I know love distortion and overdrive; if you hate distortion then I recommend amplifiers from a company called Hi-Watt. For those who love distortion I recommend getting a Marshall, Vox AC30, or an Orange amplifier. I think this is also a good place to talk about the differences between overdrive, fuzz, and distortion. All three effects are often lumped in together, and many people will refer to all of them as either overdrive or forms of distortion. Overdrive is a more transparent form of electric guitar distortion; it imparts thickness and warm crunch or breakup to the sound. Many overdrives are crafted in a way that makes them incredible for blues based music. There are transparent overdrives which impact your signal in a lighter and less obvious way; there are also overdrives which are far more opaque. All of this has to do with the clipping circuits found inside the overdrive pedals; harder clipping will yield a harsher sound while softer clipping will yield a more organic sound. Fuzz effects use germanium transistors, and sometimes tubes to add a fuzzy tone to your signal. The beauty of fuzz is that depending on the setting you have it on, the fuzz will either overdrive your signal, distort it, or add soaring amounts of sustain. Sustain is the word we use to describe how long a note or chord rings out for on electric guitar once struck; the more sustain there is the longer the note will ring out. Fuzz effects were among the first guitar pedals created, and if you want a good idea of what fuzz can sound like listen to the opening guitar riff of "Satisfaction" by The Rolling Stones. The final effect in this group is outright distortion. Distortion is exactly as the name suggests: distorting to a signal in a fundamental way. Electric guitar distortion is obvious and harsh; there is no such thing as transparent distortion. This is achieved by 'hard clipping' the circuit. So what does this mean? Your guitar outputs a signal which looks like a series of cresting, rounded waves. Hard clipping 'chops off' the rounded tops of those waves, and leaves them in a more square-like shape. These square waves sound harsh, abrasive, and metallic; if you are interested in playing heavy metal music then hard clipping distortion is your best friend. Even though I have outlined the differences between overdrive, distortion and fuzz above; the real world is not so black and white. Many distortion effects will blur the line, and cross the water into other territory; you will find overdrive or fuzz pedals that can also distort at certain settings for example. Personally, I like to 'stack' my distortion style effects; meaning I have a separate fuzz pedal, and a separate overdrive pedal and I engage them simultaneously to create entirely unique distorted tones. A word of caution though: distortion as a whole is very genre dependent. You do not want to use a hard clipping, saturated, harsh distortion pedal for the blues or soft rock. Similarly, you would not want to use a transparent and mild overdrive effect if you were playing modern heavy metal music. Some of you may not even care for any of these and will prefer to push your amp into breakup, overdrive, or distortion in a natural way by cranking up the volume on your tube amp.

35. GUITAR EFFECTS

Guitar effects come in many different shapes, flavors, and sizes. These effects are made to drastically enhance, and alter your guitar tone. Some of the most common effects are: overdrive, distortion, fuzz, phaser, boost, compression, EQ, chorus, delay, tremolo, reverb, vibrato, leslie-style effects, and wah-wah. Overdrive, distortion, boost, and fuzz all add crunch and distortion which are hallmarks of rock music. Delay, reverb, and chorus add more ethereal and ambient noises to your guitar signal; these modulation style effects are beautiful and spacey. Compression & EQ are both tone shaping tools that impact how much, and what parts of your guitar signal are emphasized; if you are a country musician compression is a must for that snappy tone. Wah-wah is an effect which is primarily used in funk, but appears in classic rock, blues and country as well; the quintessential funk tone is a wah-wah pedal with a phaser effect. Tremolo is an interesting effect that has a wide array of uses; tremolo is a volume shifting effect, but it is not that simple. Tremolo is one of the cornerstones of surf rock music, but depending on the setting it can be used in anything from swamp rock, country, and electronica. Finally, leslie-style effects such as the classic Uni-Vibe, and other chorus-vibrato effects modulate and phase the signal to create warbling-space effects, and acoustic timbres. I strongly suggest going on youtube to get a better idea of what all of these sound like. Spend a lot of time researching the effects you want before you buy them; there may be only a dozen or more categories, but the possibilities are endless. Currently, there are hundreds of thousands, potentially millions, of different takes on effects and guitar pedals.

36. PEDAL PLACEMENT

Guitar effects almost always come in a pedal format; a pedal is a small box which sits at your feet, and has a footswitch for turning the effect on or off. Guitarists will assemble a handful of their favorite effects together onto a board known as a pedal board. This is where it gets tricky; in order for your guitar tone to sound incredible there is a specific formula to follow. Here is the formula: Tuner pedals always go first, wah-style effects go next, compressor effects are third, fuzz/boost/overdrive and distortion effects are fourth in the chain, then uni-vibe style effects, phaser, modulation and reverb should be your final effect in the chain. If you are using a looper pedal the looper goes dead last, right after the reverb. Some people will change the order of these effects to get a 'unique' tone, and there is nothing wrong with that; art is art after all, but in my experience the traditional order sounds best. Whenever I have strayed from this order my guitar tone sounded washed up, warbled, and muddy. Other things you need to be mindful of are the physical size of the pedals, electrical requirements, pedalboard construction, and noise reduction. One of the worst things you can do is to get pedals which do not play nice together, and thus create a lot of unwanted electrical noise. Appropriate power solutions are also essential; no one wants to buy a $300 pedal, and find that it has been destroyed by poor power solutions. Place your pedals in such a way that the cables connecting the pedals do not cross with power cables; if they end up crossing they will act like a radio antennae, and pick up unwanted frequencies. Make sure that you understand the electrical requirements of the pedals you are using. Some guitar pedals are powered using center-negative electrical cables; others are powered using center-positive electrical cables. Screwing this up may not only cause damage to your valuable guitar equipment, but can also cause a fire.

37. GET GOOD CABLES

You would be shocked and appalled to find out just how many guitar cables are awful! Poor design and cheap components are to blame here. One of the biggest things you can do to improve the tone of your electric guitar, without breaking the bank, is to invest in good cables. This is a huge deal, bad cables will not just give you poor tone; they will crack, pop, and send very loud abrasive noises through your amp…...no one wants that! My personal favorites are Lava cables and Mogami Gold cables. Make sure that the cables you are buying are soldered; do not buy the solderless kind.

38. MASTER VIBRATO & STRING BENDING

There are certain qualities which are unique to each instrument, or certain types of instruments. The Guitar is no different: vibrato and string bending are where the guitar truly shines. Vibrato is achieved by using your finger to rapidly vibrate the string, and string bending is achieved by bending the string to the desired pitch. Both vibrato and string bending give the guitar a vocal-like quality; they are what allow the guitar to weep, cry, and scream. This is something I would go to someone in real life to physically learn; you are going to want the physical feedback of another person to help you out here.

39. LEARN TO SOLDER

Electric guitars are wonderful devices, but they are fickle and have internal components which are thin, flimsy, and subject to constant breakage. Learning to solder will go a long way in remedying these problems without paying for costly repairs. Soldering will also allow you to craft custom length guitar cables for your pedalboard and guitar. The other option is visiting a guitar or amp tech every single time a small issue occurs with pickup wiring or a jack. I should also probably point out that you will need a good amp and guitar tech for more serious issues, so definitely go out and find one in your area. Working on amplifiers can be very dangerous; I strongly urge you never to try to work on them at home, unless you are an electrician. Remedy small guitar problems at home, but send the amp to the trained professionals.

40. ARTICULATION & DYNAMICS MATTER SO MUCH MORE ON ELECTRIC GUITAR

One of the first tips I gave you in this book was to learn palm muting very early on. Palm muting matters even more on the electric guitar; the electric guitar is an extremely loud and sensitive instrument. Anything and everything you will do on an electric guitar will sound through the amplifier, and if you do not palm mute the strings you are not playing they will ring out. Palm muting can also be used to create percussive timbres on your electric guitar. Digging in the pick harder, or easing off to make your picking softer will also impact the tone of the instrument; especially, if you are using expressive or natural pedals which pick up on these pick dynamics. Hammer ons are another articulation technique which are incredibly important; to execute a hammer on bring your finger down hard on the string you want to hit. Hammering on a note does not require you to pick the note, but many guitarists will pick one note on the string then hammer onto the next note. Pull-offs are essentially the same maneuver in reverse: strike the string you want and remove your fingers in sequence. Sliding to other notes is another extremely useful and popular technique. When sliding from note to note, or chord to chord make sure you are gripping the strings with the same force, but do not white-knuckle the strings. Practice your sliding enough to make sure your fingers do not move to the wrong positions when you slide, and try practicing sliding your barre chords. All of these articulation and dynamic techniques are extremely important to learn and master.

41. EVERYTHING YOU WANT IS ON THE OTHER SIDE OF FEAR

In the beginning every guitarist has insane amounts of anxiety and fear that all have to do with playing with other musicians. I am here to tell you to let go of that fear, and just go for it. One of the biggest things you can do to improve your playing is to play with others. Other musicians will help to improve your rhythm, timing, live performance, and overall musical ability. The musical community is open and full of people who are willing to help…..if you are willing to meet them half-way. If you have done everything you were supposed to up until now then you will have the competence to be able to jam with others. If someone gives you a tip or a trick then utilize it, make an effort to learn, and people will be happy to help you. Make sure that you are honest about your musical ability with other musicians, don't lie and sign up for things you cannot do. If you are invited to be a part of a musical collaboration show up to rehearsal on-time, and never miss a rehearsal unless it is an absolute emergency. The same work ethic you show for an employment commitment is the same work ethic you should show for performance, and playing with others.

42. LEARN THE NASHVILLE NUMBER SYSTEM

This is a MUST. The Nashville number system is a universal language that allows musicians to communicate chord progressions on the fly using a system of upper and lower case roman numerals. This is the Nashville number sequence:

I = The root chord

ii= 2nd chord (always minor)

iii= 3rd chord (always minor)

IV= 4th chord (subdominant)

V= 5th chord (Dominant chord)

vi= 6th chord (always minor)

vii*= 7th chord (Diminished)

The sequence then goes back to the 1 chord, also known as the root chord of that particular root sequence. Understanding this system and how to use it is absolutely essential if you want to play with others, or play professionally. Learning this system will simplify your life immensely, and your fellow musicians will appreciate that you know the lingo and proper communication techniques.

43. DO NOT PLAY THE SAME THING THE OTHER GUITARIST IS PLAYING

There will be many times when you are playing with a fellow guitarist; suppose the other guitarist plays an open A major chord, what do you do? You have several options: you can play an A minor or major pentatonic scale, you can play notes from the relative minor scale of A major (F# minor), you can play notes from the A major scale or any of its modes. You can also find that same A major chord somewhere else on the neck, and play that voicing of the chord while the other guitarist plays the open version. No matter what you choose to do make sure that you are not playing the same exact thing the other guitarist is playing. Playing the same thing the other guitarist is playing will sound cheap and out of time. Rhythmic, melodic, and harmonic movement are products of different musicians doing different things, not the same thing.

44. STAY OUT OF YOUR FELLOW MUSICIANS JAMZONE

This goes hand in hand with the previous tip. Stay out of your fellow musicians jamzone. What do I mean by this? If the other musicians are playing in a lower register consider doing something in a higher register and vice versa. Try to contrast what you are doing, but do it tastefully. If the other guitarist is going for a solo stay out of their way; let them perform their solo. If the singer is in the middle of a passage compliment them, but do not dull their shine. So much of this is just good taste, and good jam etiquette. Here is a related tip: dynamics matter even more when playing with others. The softness or the loudness of your playing should be varied, and it should make sense. Do not start off by wailing as hard and as fast as you can on your guitar; doing this will leave you no place to go. Starting off a song with percussive palm muting, and then progressively getting louder until you reach an emotional crescendo, and come back down to a softer tone, is a far better choice.

45. UNDERSTAND THE NON-VERBAL COMMUNICATION OF OTHER PLAYERS

Have you ever seen guitarists swinging their guitars down in sync? I bet you have; this swinging down of the guitars in sync signals that the song is going to end on that note. Professional and intermediate musicians use non-verbal communication to signal each other during jam sessions and live performances. Most of the time a nod will indicate a key change, or it can mean that the player is signaling you to perform a solo. Different groups will use different non-verbals, so be sure you understand the non-verbals of the group you are playing with.

46. PRACTICE WITH A DRUMMER

One of the things that many guitarists initially overlook is jamming well with a drummer. Playing with a drummer will not be like playing with a backing track, a click track, or a metronome. This is not obvious at first, but once you play with a drummer you will understand. For this reason, and many others, it pays to spend time practicing with a drummer. Practicing with a drummer may even be more important than practicing with other guitarists. I know of many bands with only one guitarist; I do not know a single band without a drummer. Practicing with a drummer will get your rhythm tight, and your timing right.

47. DON'T LOSE COUNT

Never lose count when you are playing with others. Always keep your picking hand moving in time while palm muting the strings to keep them quiet. This is how you stay in time even when you are not playing. This also ties into many of the points mentioned above; you as a guitarist do not want to play the entire time non-stop. Playing the entire time non-stop is very tiring, and I am sure that the audience will not appreciate it either. The notes you choose not to play in music are every bit as important as the notes you do decide to play; in the immortal words of Alan Watts: "silence is what gives rise to music."

48. TRY TO LEARN NEW AND UNIQUE CHORD VOICINGS

Chord voicings are the different shades or variations of the same chord. These voicings are played in different areas on the neck. Voicings can be inversions of chords, barre shapes, shell chords, or power chords. The more of these different voicings you know the more versatile you will be as a guitarist. We saw in previous examples that we as guitarists always want to compliment or contrast other players; we never want to imitate them. Understanding where different voicings are, and how they work will turn you into a professional grade rhythm guitar player.

49. LEARN TO MIC AN AMP PROPERLY

There are different places where a microphone can be placed in relation to a guitar amplifier. Placing these microphones closer to the center of the speaker cone will result in a brighter sound. Placing the microphones closer to the edge of the speaker will introduce more low-end frequencies into the mix. Some people like to place the microphone roughly 10 inches away from the amplifier; this gives a more rounded, yet thinner tone. Much of this depends on the amp, the microphone, the venue, and personal preference. This goes hand in hand with dialing in your sound. Most amps are not meant to be cranked up all the way...neither is your guitar. Using a combination of low guitar volume, the sweet spot on your amp, overdrive pedals, and microphones will really do wonders for your tone. This matters even more in a studio where recording on lower wattage amps 5-18W is preferable, and microphones are being used to make the amp louder.

50. KNOW HOW TO USE A DIGITAL AUDIO WORKSTATION

Digital audio workstations, or DAW for short, are powerful software suites which turn your computer into a studio platform. The most popular DAW today is Protools by Apple. Guitarists in the 21st century need to know their way around a DAW. This recording knowledge helps your fellow musicians and yourself. Have an idea that you want to record? You need to be able to use the DAW. Want to send over an idea you have already recorded to a friend? Again, the DAW is indispensable. I am not saying you have to go out and become a recording engineer, but at least know the basics. Know how to connect & record instruments, adjust the EQ, compress audio properly, export files properly, add or remove studio effects in the mix.

OTHER HELPFUL RESOURCES

Tony's Acoustic Challenge

If you need structured beginners lessons this is definitely the place to go: https://tonypolecastro.com/

Signals Music Studio

This is an excellent free youtube resource. This is the channel which has the basic interval training, though the videos are not in a single playlist, so you will have to make your own playlist. The interval charts are also available as links in the description of the first video.

https://www.youtube.com/channel/UCRDDHLvQb8 HjE2r7_ZuNtWA

MuseScore 3

Here is a link to the free music transcribing software I mentioned in an earlier tip https://musescore.org/en/3.0

READ OTHER

50 THINGS TO KNOW

BOOKS

50 Things to Know

Stay up to date with new releases on Amazon:

https://amzn.to/2VPNGr7

50 Things to Know

We'd love to hear what you think about our content! Please leave your honest review of this book on Amazon and Goodreads. We appreciate your positive and constructive feedback. Thank you.

Printed in Great Britain
by Amazon